Donna Brandes and
Howard Phillips

Gamesters' Handbook

140 Games for Teachers
and Group Leaders

Stanley Thornes (Publishers) Ltd

First published by The Growth Centre (Tyneside)
54 St George's Terrace, Newcastle-upon-Tyne 1977

Published by Hutchinson in ring-binder 1978

Paperback first published by Hutchinson 1979
Reprinted 1979, 1980 (twice), 1981, 1982, 1983 (twice),
1985, 1986, 1987, 1988, 1989

Reprinted 1990 by
Stanley Thornes (Publishers) Ltd
Ellenborough House
Wellington Street
CHELTENHAM GL50 1YD

Reprinted 1992, 1993, 1994, 1995

ISBN 0 7487 0341 1

Printed and bound in Great Britain
by TJ Press (Padstow) Ltd, Cornwall

Contents

Introduction

Games Games Games

The games in this book offer a valuable source of activities, exercises and strategies for parents, group leaders, people planning parties, travellers, in fact for anyone who might wish to enliven any occasion they choose. Anyone can use the games since they can be used with different levels of skill. They can be used either simply, just for fun and enjoyment, or with greater point promoting specific aims.

The ability of many of our games to help people relax socially on both a one-to-one basis and with a group, encourages the use of the games by teachers and group leaders. This use is further enhanced by aims noted on each activity and outlining the value of the game in different developmental directions.

Games in school

Games offer flexibility: flexibility of approach, of programme, of aims. It is through this flexibility that a serious attempt can be made to develop an all round programme of personal growth. Particular aims can be fulfilled through the use of specific games in controlled directions. These can be integrated in a general plan which can then give the teacher an overall view of what is happening and what is being developed within their subject.

Games can be used constructively and not as a series of stop gap lessons or as pointless activities. Each game can have a different purpose which can always be defined — even 'fun' is purposeful.

Games can sort out problems, the kind of problems found in inter-personal relationships. They can help social inadequacy by developing co-operation within groups; develop sensitivity to the problems of others through games needing trust, and promote inter-dependency as well as an independence of personal identity.

Games can help break down artificial barriers between subjects. Simulation and improvisations provide an opportunity to extend links between subject or interest areas, and games can act as a catalyst for this. Role playing through games can extend their use in any number of directions in all subjects. Adapting games to suit a particular use is easy, especially for those familiar with 'Drama' teaching: care must be taken, however, to vary the games 'menu' and not continually dish up the same old meal with a different garnish. The size of the games selection should be useful here.

Games generate interest: they need enthusiasm. Used with purpose and effect they can be the framework upon which all other work is developed.

Games for groups

Games offer the promotion of effective communication. The usefulness of games in this direction cannot be over-emphasised. By helping people to relax in groups, games can promote the flow of communication between complete strangers and particularly shy people who need added encouragement. Additionally, hostilities can be broken down and undesirable barriers removed.

During the development of group work, games can be used in an impromptu way to extend or clarify a particular area of response. By introducing a game, the group leader can add positive reinforcement to previous ideas or add divergent ideas through analogy.

Many group discussions can be hindered by lack of 'focus'. A well chosen game can add focus to a topic or development area. This also has the added effect of stimulating the development in a refreshing way.

The added attraction in the 'role playing' aspects of many games give group members more security in which to develop their ideas and express themselves. Therefore, games can provide readily adaptable structures in which the ideas of the participants can experience growth gradually within the experience of the game and the shelter of its format.

Finally the enjoyment which can be generated by games does more than anything to develop a group identity. This fun can act as the basic ingredient for any group work and can develop cohesion and an open, accepting atmosphere much more readily than any other way.

Groups need games.

The Handbook

In compiling the games we have tried to include selections from different areas of our work so that the user can benefit from our collective classroom experience (25 years teaching) and Donna's extensive training and experience in group dynamics and Gestalt therapy. The games themselves can be used easily without any previous specialised knowledge. Each one has been found to work successfully in a number of different situations.

To further aid the developmental aspect of the games we have included a section outlining our basic teaching strategies used in conjunction with the games. The purpose of the basic strategies is to develop greater independence of action together with a realisation of the responsibility that this brings personally and socially.

We have sectioned the game into four main types:
Social, Personal, Concentrative and Introductory.

The sections, however, are to be used only as a guide. Many of the games have a number of uses, some of which transcend specified sections. The games, therefore, are sectionalised for the benefit of the user through bias only and not through any strict division of material. Social and Personal Development sections are self explanatory in their material. The Introductory section is used primarily for warm up exercises, but also for concluding activities too. Because of this they are often quite short. Concentrative games are used when people need to focus their attention on either a mental or a physical problem requiring skilful development.

The Handbook itself is used simply. Games can be chosen from each alphabetical section and can be used either in conjunction with one another, or independently. The games can be detached from the handbook and used separately. If this is to be done regularly we recommend that you reinforce favourite games with gummed rings or strips of transparent adhesive tape. Teachers might also like to use the games number on their record sheets so that a greater diversification of materials can be used.

Acknowledgement of sources

We have been using these games in our work with many kinds of groups. They have grown with us over the years, and their sources have been wide and various. Their growth has also involved adaptation, evolution, integration, extension, variation, so that it is no longer possible to identify sources for most of the games. Games can not be copyrighted, so that our own games, as well as games which we have obtained from other books, are open for use by anyone. Many times we have "invented" a game for an occasion, only to find it later in a book, and vice versa.

Among the books which have been most useful to us are those of Sidney Simon, William Schutz, John Stevens.

We are especially indebted to Steve Myers, of Mt. View, California, for his pioneering work in Human Development in schools.

Basic strategies

The waiting game

This approach removes a great deal of the need for discipline and attention getting devices on the part of the teacher. Tell the group that you are not going to fight for their attention or quiet, that whenever they are together as a group for instruction or discussion, you will just wait until they are ready to listen. Tell them that it is called 'The Waiting Game', and that you will not take the responsibility for their attention, that they must take it themselves. (Note: I have seen this used with very small children, five year olds. After the first few lessons, they will get themselves and each other quiet, with no reminders from the leader).

The leader's waiting must have a quality of nothingness..... no resignation or martyred patience: all questions and interruptions must be ignored. It must be a non-threatening attitude as well; do not worry about the time you are wasting. If you persevere with them in the beginning, you will save great quantities of time and effort later.

Remember, the idea behind the Waiting Game is that the group takes all responsibility for how they are behaving, not the leader. If they use Drama time at first to chat with each other, they will soon get bored and express a preference for active happenings. So think of something else while you are waiting, plan your dinner menus or tomorrow's lesson or recite 'How do I love thee? Let me count the ways'.

You must be patient and consistent and play it every time, or it will not work.

'The circle' or 'rounds'

Sitting in a circle, rather than in rows of chairs or in a random setting, can influence group dynamics. It gives everyone the same status, including the leader, and it exposes each one's face to everyone else, and allows eye contact: therefore, a great many activities in this compendium are played or experienced in a circle.

The circle must be understood and experienced as a safe place, a place where one can speak freely about his opinions or feelings without the risk of being laughed at or judged.

Therefore, when groups are sitting in the circle, the leader must make sure that the freedom of the situation is understood to be contained in a safe structure.

A 'round' is a time when each person in the circle, progressing around the circle in turn, makes a statement completing one of the following sentences (or others of your own devising):
I noticed .... (particularly good for films, etc.)
I discovered .... (especially after a new experience or game)
I wish ....
I learned ....

Resent and Appreciate .... this is highly recommended for evaluation of an experience. One round of 'I resent ....', followed by a round of 'I appreciate' ...., for negative and positive feelings, in that order.

When doing rounds, everyone who is not actually the speaker, must listen quietly, and no comments are to be made, even by the leader. If a statement is made which does necessitate discussion, this should be saved until after the rounds are completed. Anyone can refuse a turn by saying: 'I pass', and there should be no comment about this either.

This structure can be used for many purposes, including the following:
Evaluation
To discuss an experience, a film, a play, a game just played
Planning, class meetings, problem solving
Positive reinforcement   **10**

Brainstorming

The object of brainstorming is to generate a great many useful ideas on any subject or problem in a short period of time; it is also very useful for producing possible material for writing or discussion.

Suppose a class is looking for potential places to take a field trip. The leader places a blackboard at the front of the group, and asks for ideas. He writes down every idea, without comment, discarding nothing. If ideas are slow to come, he can put some of his own down, but he should wait before doing so. Once the ideas begin coming, they tend to come very quickly.

When ideas have stopped flowing, he stops writing, and pointing to each asks how many people think that that one has possibilities, erasing the ones that have no votes at all, unless someone wants to discuss them. Now the remaining possibilities are discussed in detail, and finally one is chosen by voting.

Remember:
No negative evaluation of any idea is to be made by the leader.
Work for quantity, not quality: the longer the list, the better.
Encourage zany, far-out ideas.

A secondary objective for brainstorming is to unite the group.This happens, usually, if the brainstorming session is properly led, because each person has had a chance to contribute, and is made to feel that his idea is at least worth writing down. It turns group problem-solving away from a competitive atmosphere where people are contending to have their own ideas accepted, and towards a collaborative venture where the problem itself is the prime adversary, and not another member of the group.

If a group has not experienced brainstorming before, it is a good idea to introduce it with the following games:

Coke bottle

Leader has blackboard and chalk, or large chart paper and felt pen.

Leader says: 'Imagine that you are on a desert island. There is plenty of food and shelter, but only one man-made object, a COCA-COLA bottle. Using your wildest imaginations, think of as many uses as you possibly can for that coke bottle'. The leader then writes down the ideas as fast as group members can call them out, omitting none, and writing them completely at random so that no ranking is possible. No one should comment on any ideas until all of them are written. The leader can also put in ideas, thus remaining a contributing member of the group.

1001 uses of a shoe

Same as above, but an element of competition is introduced by brainstorming in teams (using a shoe instead of a coke bottle, as this game is often used as a follow-up to 'Coke Bottle'). Each team is given a leader, paper and pencil, and three minutes to brainstorm, then their ideas are counted. Another two minutes, and count the total. One last minute period, and the total for each team is announced. The teams then are allowed a few minutes to come to a group decision about which are their five most original ideas, i.e. the ones that the other team will not have. The teams sit together and read the five they have chosen. Points are given for any ideas which have not been thought of by any other team.

Ask them policy

Whatever problems or concerns you are having with any given group, they are not your problems, they are the group's problems: do not try to solve them at home in bed at night, or in the staff room. Tell the problem to the group and ask for ideas or feelings about it. Remember, you are as much a member of the group as anyone else; you should share your feelings and problems with them if you want real group interaction.

Social development

Contents

S1   Air-raid shelter

Materials   None

Aims   Role-playing, group decision-making, group interaction.

Procedure   Divide in groups of 8 — 10. Each group member adopts a specific role, usually an occupation, e.g. a doctor, an athlete, a teacher, movie-star, mother, housewife, etc. (These can be written out and picked from a hat). Tell groups they are in an air-raid shelter after an atom bomb has fallen, big enough and with enough air and food for only six people, therefore they must get rid of several members. Each group member must argue as to why he should be allowed to survive. A group decision must be reached as to who goes and stays: no suicides or murder allowed. Set a time limit for the decision. Later discuss how the group interacted making the decision, whether each person played an active or passive role, how satisfied each was with his role, etc.

Variations   Instead of an air-raid shelter, have a life raft or desert island or space ship. Add incidents, accidents, rituals, funerals, ceremonies.

S2 Backward fall & catch

Materials   None

Aims   Trust development, relaxation

Procedure   Partners stand at a relative distance, one person behind the other, but both facing the same direction. The person in front allows himself to fall back and be caught by his rear partner. The front person must be relaxed. Distance can be varied within a safe limit.

Variations   One person stands between two and falls backwards and forwards. The person is propelled to an upright position each time. To be successful the subject must be relaxed.

Group of about six or seven stand in close circle. Subject stands in the centre and allows himself to fall backwards and forwards, sideways, etc. Participants may gently propel subject into the upright position, or towards another member of the circle. It is important that the subject stays in the centre and that he is relaxed with eyes closed and feet stationary.

S3 **Body lift**

Materials   None

Aims   Trust, concentration, group development

Procedure   Group chooses each member in turn and elevates them to a horizontal position above the heads of the group. The person is held there for a specific period, and then lowered carefully to the floor. The elevated person must relax and close eyes.

It is often a good idea to have the groups raise and lower in unison. This often avoids confusion and helps concentration.

Variations   Vary speed and control of lift, — walk, rock, etc. Have the person involved give instructions to the group. Combine with S2 Backward fall & catch.

S4

Clay Island

Materials　Enough clay for each group of seven people to gather around a round or square table and work together. Clay should be malleable, non-drying variety; also leaves, twigs and tooth-picks, or sticks should be provided.

Aims　Group interaction, role playing, creativity.

Procedure

a Groups of 5 — 7 gather around a table or on the floor with a large lump of clay in the centre. Spend 10 minutes pounding, pushing, slapping clay into large, soft, formless mass. Encourage energetic pounding of the clay. Together, form the lump into an island, adding terrain, coves, caves, mountains, rivers. (Non-verbal).

b Without talking, stake out a territory on the island for yourself, mark boundaries, build a shelter or home, and improve as desired.

c Hold an island council meeting, elect leader, make whatever decisions group deems necessary for survival or interaction on the island. (Give these directions one step at a time).

Can stop here and go into discussion of the group interaction, or go further (see variations).

Variations　Continue with small groups, improvising incidents of island life. Can be done with large paper and chalk instead of clay.

S5 **Conveyor belt**

Materials   None

Aims   Trust, group development

Procedure   Two lines of people facing each other (about two feet apart).
Try to have people of similar height opposite. First couple
detach and one person lies on back between first six/eight
people. The person is lifted to head height and is then slowly
passed down the whole length of the chain. The person is
carefully lowered to the ground at the end. Better results
if the person relaxes and closes eyes.

S6   # D.U.E. Depth unfolding experience

Materials   None

Aims   Trust building, self-disclosure, getting to know each other

Procedure   Groups of no more than eight. Each person has six minutes
                to talk about himself. Emphasise those things you
                particularly would like new people to know about you. (No
                feedback is given at this time.) Afterwards, use a group
                interview, or a feedback session giving first impressions, or a
                strength bombardment.

S7   # Fear in a hat

Materials   Pencil, paper, 'hat' (or tin, etc.)

Aims   Share and accept

Procedure   Played in a circle. Ask everyone, including leader, to complete this sentence: (anonymously) 'In this class (or group, or whatever) I am afraid that ....' Put the scraps of paper in the tin or receptacle in the centre. Pass the tin around, stopping at each person while he draws one out and reads it, enlarging on the sentence and trying to express what the person was feeling. (For example, the leader reads the first one, and might say 'In this class I am afraid that I will be laughed at ....(continues talking) I am afraid to say my feelings because everyone laughs at me, so I never say anything.') Continue around the circle. Leader must make sure that everyone just listens, and does not comment. No arguing or comment is allowed. Then discuss what was noticed or discovered.

Variations   Likes and dislikes in a hat (two tins)

Worries in a hat

Gripes in a hat

Wishes in a hat, etc.

S8   Group interview

self-disc

Materials   None

Aims   Trust building, self-disclosure, self-awareness, reflective listening.

Procedure   Sit in a circle, one volunteer is the focus of the group. Anyone may ask any questions of the focal person. He may answer honestly, or say 'I'd rather not answer that.' The purpose of the questions should be to get to know the person on a more than superficial level. Questioners tend to become more skilful with experience. Leader must work to prevent the group from arguing or criticizing the focal person — it is just time to listen and accept. Leader can direct the questions to a deeper level than just biographical facts by asking questions which require thought, philosophy, opinions, feelings, etc. A possible closing question is: 'Is there something else you'd like us to know about you?' Continue as long as group maintains interest. Interview other members throughout the course.

Variations   Do rounds of questions. Do short interviews of several people. Let everyone be the focus at once, ask each other questions.

S9   **Guess who said it**   *feedback*

Materials   None

Aims   Give and accept positive feedback, trust building

Procedure   Played in a circle. One person leaves the room. Three or
four people make positive statements about him,
trying to include specialised information that not everyone
might know about the person. When he returns, he stands
in a circle, and the statements are repeated to him one at a
time, while he tries to guess who said each one. (Leader
insists on receiving only positive statements).

S10

Head rest & roll

Materials   None

Aims   Trust, concentration, relaxation

Procedure   One partner lies on the floor and relaxes. Other partner supports his head and slowly manipulates it from left to right. Prone partner must allow his neck muscles to relax and be fully supported. (very difficult) Care must be taken that trust is broad-based in this activity. Successes in this difficult activity must be noted.

feedback

S11   It's obvious

Materials   None

Aims   Trust building, awareness of how we look at other people, ice-breaker.

Procedure   Break into groups of 4 or 5, sit in a small circle with your group. Focus on one person, have each person in the group look at A and start a sentence with 'It's obvious that you......' Make sure it is something obvious, like an item of clothing — no inferences allowed here. Do the same for B, C, D etc. Start again, take a closer look, start a sentence with 'I see that you.......' This would be something that you might not notice at first glance, but only on looking more closely. Go all the way around. Start again with 'I imagine that you.......' Here you are allowed guesses, inferences, wild imaginings. Check the imaginings with the focal person: 'Is that right?' Discuss the experience in the small groups. Join the large group for a round of 'I discovered ....'

Variations   Do more imaginings about other people in your group. Write down the imaginings.

S12   Mental gifts

Materials   Pencil, two or three small pieces of paper each

Aims   Trust building, positive feedback, learning to give and take compliments or suggestions.

Procedure   **a** (If large blackboards are available.)
Write each group member's name at the top of a section of the board. Everyone walks around writing mental gifts in each person's section. They should be something you think the person would like, or something you think they should have. Example: 'I give you the gift of appreciating your own wisdom'.

       b (If no blackboards)
Everyone writes his name on four or five scraps of paper. These are put into a hat or dish: each member draws five out and addresses gifts to those names. At a signal everyone delivers their gifts. They can be shared aloud, if desired.

Variations   1 On festive occasions, pre-cut Valentine hearts, paper Christmas trees, Easter eggs, etc., to write the gifts on.

       2 Repeat this at intervals during the course. Try to see that gifts become more relevant to the needs of the receiver.

S13   **Parties**

Materials   None

Aims   Characterisation, improvisation

Procedure   Have improvisation of rich people's parties, poor people's parties, students' parties, re-unions (e.g. jail breakers' re-unions, any re-unions, etc.) It is a good idea to have the group decide what kind of a party it wants. Each person (or with a partner) decides who they are and what they have to say at this party. Discuss who they are going as, what they are looking forward to doing there, etc. Have a person announce each newcomer, or pair of people, as they arrive. It is worth while discussing the whole thing afterwards with regard to:

     a   whether objective was achieved

     b   what was real/unreal about it

     c   why we interpret these kind of people in this kind of way

Variations   Develop to show racial, national, political, relationships etc.

S14   **Partner conversations**

Materials   None

Aims   Trust building, imagination, fun

Procedure   Get a partner, hold hands or put arms around each other. Find
            another pair, and hold a conversation with them, each
            partner alternating in speaking one word, until a sentence is
            formed. (It becomes an exercise in mind-reading.)

Variations   Use teams (3 or 4) instead of pairs.

S15 **Pass the buck**

Materials   The Buck (a pen, glove, pack of cigarettes, etc.)

Aims   Control group interaction, concentration

Procedure   Leader holds the Buck, says no one can speak unless they are
holding it. Pass it to the next person in the circle, or to whoever raises his hand to speak.

Variations   Toss it quickly back and forth: *must* speak when you have it
or you are out. Use it to tell stories: whoever has the Buck
must continue.

Social development
Communication
Movement, body skills
Warm-up, ice-breaker
Trust, sensitivity

S16 **Pile-up**

Materials   None

Aims   Warm up, group development, trust

Procedure   Members of the group lie on their stomachs and close their eyes. All start crawling towards central point and they meet. They crawl over each other until pile starts to form in the centre. When pile is complete, all open eyes.

Variations   Blindfold 'bumps': Group is blindfolded and walks to the centre to form a knot.

S17 **Resent & appreciate**

Materials   None

Aims   Evaluation, problem solving, expression of feeling, trust building.

Procedure   **a** In a circle. Each person makes a statement beginning with 'I resent ......' (ordinarily, in relation to the work just completed, or the experience in the class or group.)

b Repeat the round, beginning with 'I appreciate......'

c Before starting, make sure that everyone understands the meaning of both words. *No one is allowed to comment.*

d Anyone can say 'I pass', which means 'No comment.'

e Anyone can say: 'I resent nothing', or 'I appreciate nothing.'

Note   This is not an ordinary game, but a most crucial one. It is used for evaluation purposes throughout any course or group work.

S18 **The rule of the game**

Materials   None

Aims   Group interaction, imagination, intellectual exercise, fun,
                   getting to know each other.

Procedure   Circle: one person goes out, others choose a rule. When he
                   comes back he must find out the rule by asking people
                   questions about themselves. A good rule to begin with:
                   answer every question as if you were the person on your
                   right. Players must answer questions honestly, according to
                   the rules. Another example: all girls tell lies, all men tell the
                   truth.

                   Rules can be hard or very simple, according to age and
                   experience. Rules can be visual (scratch head before
                   answering), or structural (each answer begins with the next
                   letter of the alphabet).

S19 **Sabotage**

Materials   None

Aims   Awareness of group dynamics, breaking down barriers, trust building, empathy. Good opening exercise.

Procedure

a Discuss meaning of sabotage as opposed to destruction (sabotage is subtle, covert).

b Do a round of: 'I could sabotage this group by.......' or, do a round of things we say that sabotage ourselves, e.g. 'I'm too tired, 'I've done this before'.

c Divide in threes. A tells B one of his own problems. B just listens, nods, encourages. B does *not* try to solve problem). C tries to sabotage the communication, interrupts, etc., trying to be as subtle as possible. Change roles until each has experienced each role. Do a round of: 'I discovered.......'

d Do a round of: 'I could help this group by.......', or, things we say that help us to be part of the group, e.g. 'Today I'll really listen.'

Variations   Use non-verbal sabotage, or invent other forms.

S20   # Sitting circle

Materials   Circle of over 25 people

Aims   Trust, fun

Procedure
a   Group stands in a close circle, in queue form, with right shoulders towards the centre of the circle.

b   Circle closes so that everyone is touching the person in front and behind them.

c   Participants hold the waist of the person in front

d   Everyone bends their knees until they feel themselves supported on the knee of the person behind.

e   If successful (rare first time) the whole group is self-supported, each person sitting on the knee of the person behind.

Note   This can only be successful if the circular shape is maintained throughout and it is helpful if the group leans *slightly* towards the centre as they are trying to settle down.

Variations   *After secure sitting position is achieved*

1   Everyone leans inwards slightly and raises left leg

2   All stretch arms in unison

3   Try alternate stepping with right and left feet, (very difficult.)

S21	**Structures**

Materials   None

Aims   Trust, concentration, body control

Procedure   Leader split group into small units. Each unit (2 – 8) constructs a particular structure by linking themselves together.

Ideas   Make a suspension bridge
an arched bridge
a tree
a crane
a modern building
an aeroplane/helicopter
a car/truck/bus
a ship
an antenna
a tower
a dome
a temple
a cathedral

Variations   Move around without falling

S22

Territories

Materials   None

Aims   Values clarification, self-validation, group and social
                   development.

Procedure   Discuss how the world is broken up into different countries
                   or states, and how each state makes its own laws within its
                   boundaries. Each group or individual marks off a territory,
                   using chairs, tables, etc., and makes its own laws. After
                   discussion this can lead to various improvisations within each
                   territory. Leader can suggest that improvisation is based
                   upon someone who breaks one of the laws, or on a stranger
                   who visits the new territory, etc.

Variations   One group could become the authority in a particular state
                   and the rest of the group has to do as they are told.

                   Ideas must be worked out beforehand however, or else the
                   leader must take an active role as one of the citizens.

                   Territories can be fantasy places, outer space, etc.

S23   # Teacher-student fantasy

Materials   Small groups or pairs

Aims   Social development, improvisation, role-playing, values development

Procedure

a Each pair sits facing each other, and closes their eyes.

b Each person thinks back over his school career, and remembers the 'worst teacher he ever had'. Remember in detail, all the annoying or destructive behaviours of that teacher.

c Partners open their eyes and take turns talking to that worst teacher, using the partner as the 'target', and telling him off, saying all the things they would never dare say in person.

d Discuss that experience.

e Follow the same procedure with the 'best teacher'.

f In the large group, do a round of 'I discovered' or 'I noticed'.

Variations

1 Make the conversations into improvisations.

2 Brainstorm qualities of 'bad' and 'good' teachers.

3 Choose one of the negative qualities and follow-up on it, applying it to yourself, doing a value continuum (P58 Value Continuum).

S24	**True story**

Materials	None
Aims	Self-disclosure, trust building, listening skills
Procedure	**a** 'A' tells a partner of a true incident that happened to him
	b Partner 'B' repeats it, trying to keep the same inflection and emphasis that A had.
	c A takes on a different role, (e.g. an absent-minded old woman) and tells or enacts the story again.
	d A and B discuss the experience
	e Switch and repeat
Variations	A and B enact each others' stories

S25   **Trust walk**

Materials   Blindfolds (optional), outdoor area preferred

Aims   Trust building, sensory awareness

Procedure   Emphasise that this is a *non-verbal* experience. Choose a
partner that you would like to know better. A closes eyes
(or is blindfolded), B leads him and helps him to experience
the world around through his other four senses. Communicate with each other through touch. Protect your partner,
let him know you care, be very gentle, try to give him a truly
beautiful experience. After 15 — 30 minutes, switch roles.
After an equal time, lead your partner back here. Discuss the
experience with your partner, then join the group and do a
round of 'I discovered.......'

Variations   There are many other 'blind' experiences described elsewhere
in this collection.

S26   **Two & two make one**

Materials   None

Aims   Trust, personal development

Procedure   Leader asks the group to space out. Each person to see how
                 far he can lean over without falling. People then pair up and
                 see what a difference another's support can make in
                 repeating the exercise.

                 Discuss observations afterwards. Draw comparisons

S27   **Verbal boxing**

Materials   Stop watch or clock

Aims   Overcome shyness, warm-up for drama, fun, imagination

Procedure   One challenger faces another in the centre for a 30 second
                  bout: the group decides who has won, a third person can
                  challenge the winner.

                  'Bouts' fall into categories:

a   Insults: colourful and inventive *untrue* insults should be
         encouraged; no 'hitting below the belt' with truth or
         weakness: this is in the form of a conversation.

b   Long-windedness: the challenger must keep up a *continuous*
         stream of talk, both at the same time.

c   Gibberish: give challengers an emotion to express, (e.g. fear),
         must be expressed with nonsense sounds: both talking at
         once.

Variations   Invent new categories

S28　　　**Wall crash**

Materials　　None

Aims　　Trust, group development, self-validation, personal development.

Procedure　a　Whole group forms a queue

b　Leader chooses two people to act as safety nets, they stand near the wall opposite the queue.

c　The person at the front of the queue walks, eyes closed, towards the wall.

d　'Safety nets' catch him before he hits the wall

e　After each person has had a turn at a walking pace, the pace is speeded up on each turn, until the person is running at full speed.

The point is that the trust develops through a feeling of safety each time the person is caught by the 'safety nets', so that, in the end, he feels safe even when he is running.

S29   # What do they want?

Materials   None

Aims   Values development, social awareness, trust

Procedure   .   Start with a round and discuss the way in which people
                       group together: i.e. family, friends, school, college, housing
                       estate, town region, nation. *Also:* Religion, Politics, Race.

                       Round splits into groups of about eight. Each group forms
                       itself under one of the above categories divided in the initial
                       round.

                       Leader acts as devil's advocate and/or mediator between
                       groups. Verbal conflict is to be desired and control must be
                       exercised to maintain this: emotions are expected to run
                       high. Groups must re-assemble afterwards into a round and
                       plenty of time must be left for discussion.

Note   This strategy can be a major contribution to the development
                       of the above themes.

Variations   Smaller units can be used: i.e. partners.

S30

Whose face

Materials   Blindfolds for the whole group

Aims   Concentration, inter-personal development

Procedure   Partners sit facing each other and examine each other's
facial features, both visually and with finger tips. Gentleness
must be emphasised.

Afterwards one partner is blindfolded and they have to
discover their partner from the main group. The other
partner is then blindfolded and the activity is repeated.

Variations   Both partners are blindfolded and they have to find each
other.

S31   **Who's missing?**

Materials   Small prizes, such as sweets. (optional)

Aims   Memory training, concentration, building groups, fun.

Procedure   Group is seated, scattered around the room, one person, A,
                    goes out. The group moves around, changing places, and one
                    more person, B, leaves by the other door, or hides. A returns
                    and has 30 seconds to guess who's missing. If he does he
                    wins (a small sweet, if you wish to give prizes), if he doesn't
                    B wins.

Variations   Add consequences for the loser

S32   **The word wizard**

Materials   Pencil and paper

Aims   Imagination, communication, group interaction, fun

Procedure   (The instructions below are given slowly, and one at a time, with pauses between.)

Leader says: 'I am a wizard, I am taking away all your words. But as I am generous, you may have four of them back. Write down the four words you want to keep out of all the words in the world. Find a partner, communicate using *only* your four words, plus gestures....... (pause). Now you may share words with your partner, write down his words. Now you have up to eight words. Change partners and communicate with these words on your list only. Share words. Repeat, changing partners 4 to 6 times. Now take your list and try to write a poem using just those words.'

Personal development

Contents

P33   # Advertisements

Materials   Pencil and paper each

Aims   Self-disclosure, positive feedback, group trust building.
                   (Group should know each other a while before playing this).

Procedure   Write an advertisement describing and selling yourself as a
                   friend. (Twenty five words or less). Keep in mind: why
                   would someone want to buy (choose) you rather than
                   another friend? Put ads. in a hat, pass around, read aloud
                   one at a time, guess who wrote each (be able to say *why* you
                   guessed that person). Do a round of 'I noticed..........'

Variations   1 Advertisements of self as a parent, teacher, pupil, son/
                   daughter, brother/sister, lover, sweetheart, etc.

                   2 Put large ads. on the wall, write ads. for other people.

                   3 Illustrate or make cartoons of the ads.

P34   **Auctions**

Materials   None

Aims   Develop self-confidence, imagination

Procedure   Each member of the group decides to auction an imaginary object and after some time at individual preparation, (optional) group members improvise a sale of the object. Each member of the group should take part as an auctioneer

Variations   Class brings in articles for mock or even real auction.

P35 **Blind dinner**

Materials
Group members bring unusual foods, cut in small pieces, arranged on paper plates. Be sure there are also things to drink.

Aims
Sensory awareness, trust building, fun.

Procedure
a Sit at tables, close eyes, pass things around and sample them. *Non-verbal.*

b Spread things on large table, walk around and feed each other samples. *Non-verbal.*

c Help yourself to a plateful, sit down alone, close eyes, taste and savour samples in silence.

d Sit in circle, close eyes, have a few people passing things to taste. (See that they also get a tasting turn.)

Variations
Do several times, different ways, use foreign foods, cheese and wine, fruits and nuts, etc.

P36   # American charades

Materials   Paper, pencils, watch with second hand

Aims   Fun, communication, non-verbal communication, drama

Procedure

a   Divide into two teams and go into separate rooms

b   Write on slips of paper: song titles, film titles, books, famous people, famous sayings, plays, etc.

c   Come back into same room, sit with your team, send one person for a slip of paper from the other team.

d   Act out the title on the paper for your own team, according to the structure outlined below, while someone keeps time. After 3 minutes, time is up, and someone from the other team gets a piece of paper and tries.

e   The team with lowest time elapsed at the end, wins. So a cumulative score of minutes and seconds for each team is kept.

Structure   for acting out titles. (You cannot talk)

1   Show your team what the title is with agreed sign e.g.
movie: crank the camera
play: pull the curtains,
Everyone on your team shouts out the answers.

2   Show with fingers, number of words

3   Show with fingers, which word you are starting with

4   Fingers on wrist indicate number of syllables and also which syllable, if necessary.

5   Begin acting out words

6   Other signals can be made up and agreed upon, such as 'Little words', 'Big words', 'Whole idea', 'Shorten word', 'Lengthen word', 'Rhymes with', etc.

Lesson ②

P37   **Coat of arms**

Materials   Paper, pencils, scissors, felt pens, or chalk.

Aims   Self-awareness, self-disclosure

Procedure   Show examples of heraldry and coats of arms, discuss
symbolism. Design your own coat of arms; suggestions below
are only optional, it is best if people invent their own. (The
suggestions are also just ideas; people invent their own
symbols.) Afterwards, share and discuss.

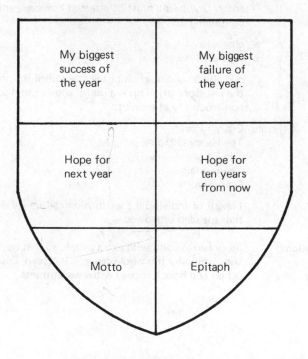

My biggest success of the year	My biggest failure of the year.
Hope for next year	Hope for ten years from now
Motto	Epitaph

Variations   Make huge ones for the whole group

P38   # Continuing story

Materials   None

Aims   Confidence, communication, imagination

Procedure   One group of about four people decide on the theme of a
                    story. They begin to develop this story and the characters
                    they have chosen. At a given point the leader substitutes four
                    other people to take over the rules of the original four and
                    continue the story. There may be slight variations in this as
                    one character may leave the story and a different one may
                    enter. One point must be stressed however, and that is
                    continuing of:

                 a character
                 b theme

                    and also a continuation of the story until the group finishes
                    the last story off. This is a useful activity to discuss
                    constructively afterwards.

Example themes   Crazy races
                    The Haunted House
                    The Escape
                    The Funfair
                    Crazy Sports

                    Length of individual contribution can be varied and story
                    thus speeded or slowed.

Variations   Story can expand with extra people so that no-one drops out
                    and eventually the whole group is included. Discuss centre of
                    action and how it moved with new entrants.

P39 ## Control tower

Materials   Blindfolds, chairs, books, other obstacles

Aims   Trust building, awareness, fun

Procedure   a   Blindfold **A** (plane): **B** (the control tower) guides him verbally through an obstacle course (runway) which has been set up between two rows of chairs.

b   **A** gets one penalty point each time he touches an obstacle.

c   When he has five points, he 'crashes', and **B** crashes with him. They are out.

d   Another pair starts; the obstacles are changed around.

Variations   Use human obstacles.   Play in teams

P40   # Don't make me laugh

Materials   None

Aims   Personal development, fun, concentration

Procedure   One partner becomes a serious character and decides he will
                      never laugh or even smile again. The other partner has to
                      change this state of affairs. The leader will have to decide
                      whether tickling, etc., is allowed. Partners exchange roles
                      when the first partner does laugh.

Variations   Make partner angry instead. No hurting though, no blows or
                      personal comments. Discuss afterwards.

P41 **Feeling cards**

Materials   Blackboard, felt pen, strips and cardboard about 3" x 7"
(brightly coloured if possible).

Aims   Become aware of feelings, learn feeling vocabulary, become
accustomed to showing and discussing feelings.

Procedure   a   Brainstorm (see 'Brainstorming' page 11) feeling words.
Leader writes these words on coloured cards.

b   Leader holds up a card, (e.g. card says 'embarrassed' or
'hateful'). Members complete sentence using word: 'I feel
embarrassed when ....'

c   Groups of three, pick words at random, make mime or short
play using all the three words (feelings).

d   Relate true experiences: 'The last time I felt really
embarrassed was when ....'

e   Speak for someone else, check accuracy. Example: (Sally is
speaking for Joan): 'I'm Joan and I feel embarrassed when
I'm asked to speak out in class. Is that true Joan?' Joan
answers and discusses Sally's statement.

Variations   1   Have people choose (or make) cards which describe their
feelings right now. Discuss.

2   Use cards to inspire essays, poetry, art; hang cards on wall.
Have members make up games using the cards.

P42   **Fists**

Materials   None

Aims   Sound relationships, self-validation

Procedure   One person in each pair closes his fists tightly and the other
                person tries to persuade him to open them. After a
                reasonable time the partners exchange roles.

Instruction   'Only open your fist if you feel you have really been
                persuaded by your partner'.

Variations 1 Partner One coils body, and the other person has to
                   straighten it out.

                2 Partner holds his own feet

                3 Partner clenches his teeth

Note   No form of violence is allowed, although threats may be
                used.

P43   **Gripes auction**

Materials   A card or piece of paper for each person and pencils

Aims   Self-validation, social development, values clarification

Procedure   The leader holds a series of cards, each containing a gripe.
(see below). All the gripes are read out first and then each
gripe is put up for auction. Each person has 100 points to
spend and cannot bid over this. When the auction is over the
people who have cards explain why their particular gripe is
important and how it affects their lives.

A sheet of paper should be reserved to note the number of
points each gripe is sold for. This is to check on the points
each person spends.

List of gripes	Dogs	Vandalism
Little children	The Weather	Drama Lessons
Baby sitting	Pocket Money	School Dances
Smokers	School Meals	Dentists
Films on T.V.	Sports	Violence
Newspapers	Cats	Television
Parents	Homework	Town Council
School	Books	Policemen
Brothers	Teachers	Fashions
Sisters	Grandparents	Shopping
Youth Club	Pollution	Doctors
Holidays		
Gossips		

Facilities for young people (recreation)

Variations   Brainstorm list of gripes first

P44   **Group yell**

Materials   None

Aims   Release tension, warm-up, trust building

Procedure   Group huddle together in crouching position. Leader begins a
                       low hum. As the group begins to rise slowly, the sound level
                       also rises, so that at the end, everyone leaps into the air and
                       shouts at the same time.

                       Repeat until everyone has really *shouted* at the end.

Variations   Add specific words or sounds chosen by the group in
                       advance.

P45   # Hell

Materials   None (although suitable music and rostrum blocks are helpful).

Aims   Improvisation, fun, group leadership, personal development

Procedure   Whole group discusses various torments and evil which abound in hell. Also the sounds and the visual impact of such a scene. Pairs and threes act various torments. Eventually (with possible music stimulus) whole group joins and the torments change partners and move among the tormented. This situation is reversed later so that everyone has been given a place on each side.

Try to improvise torments particularly suited to members of the group.

Variations   1 One person can be the devil for a day and order and direct the group.

2 Try to develop more sophisticated tensions or torments. (Relate to everyday tensions which can build up.)

3 Discuss various ideas about Heaven, and repeat the above processes.

Suitable music which can be used: Ride of the Valkyries, Rite of Spring.

P46   # I am a shoe

Materials   None

Aims   Mixing, self-disclosure, self-awareness

Procedure   Sit silently, look around the room and choose any object.
Think what it would be like to be that. Name three qualities
it possesses. (e.g. I am a shoe, I am warm, soft and
comfortable). Go around the room introducing yourself that
way and shaking hands. Now sit down, think briefly about
whether those qualities describe you. Give the object your
own name, and walk around introducing yourself that way.
(I am Susan, I am warm, soft, and comfortable.) Make a
circle and discuss the experience, doing a round of 'I felt
..........', or 'I discovered..........'

Variations   Write a story as if you were the object, or tell one aloud.
Find a partner and discuss the qualities you chose, in relation
to yourself and your partner.

P47   # Lawyer

Materials   None, chairs in a circle

Aims   Concentration, sharpening of wits, fun

Procedure   The Lawyer stands in the centre, says to the players, 'Starting now, you must not answer when I speak to you, the person on your left must answer for you. You must not nod, or smile, or respond to me in any way. Do you understand?' The players almost invariably answer, and they would be out .... The Lawyer starts again, asking each person questions and putting them out if they answer. To progress to the next rule and make it more sophisticated, no one may answer 'Yes' or 'No' .... New rules may be added as you go along.

P48   **Memory game**

Materials   A tray, with twelve assorted objects, a scarf or towel, pencil and paper.

Aims   Memory training, observation, concentration

Procedure   Leader previously has assembled twelve objects on a tray (e.g. hairbrush, stapler, clock, etc.) and covered the tray with a towel. Gather the group around, unveil the tray, and give them 30 seconds to silently observe the tray. Cover the tray and have them list as many objects as they can remember.

Variations   Give small prizes (a sweet) for the most listed. Remove one object from the tray, give a prize for the first person who can tell what is missing.

Personal development
Imagination, creativity
Communication
Movement

P49 **Merry-go-round**

Materials   None

Aims   Lead up to improvisation, role-playing, fun

Procedure   **a** Two people begin improvising a scene, on any subject. (e.g. a burglar and a policeman).
They are Number 1 and Number 2.

b After the scene is well established, any one from the audience may come up and start a new scene; he is Number 3 and must change the subject completely. (Perhaps he might be a surgeon and begin talking about the operation taking place.)

c Number 1 has to find a reason to leave, in the context of the scene, leaving Numbers 2 and 3 together.

d Number 4 comes up, changing the subject again. Number 2 finds a reason to leave.

e The game continues as long as it is fresh and lively.

P50   # News & goods

Materials   None

Aims   Warm-up, self-validation, self-disclosure, trust building

Procedure   As a round: start a sentence with 'The nicest thing that happened to me this week was ....' Emphasize that it might be something big and exciting or small and pleasant. (Perhaps just a smile from someone special.)

Variations   Write them anonymously, guess who wrote them. Sometimes do 'Bad News': 'The worst thing that happened to me this week was ....' (Follow this with 'Good News'.). Sometimes do Bad News and discuss the degree of sympathy desired.

Personal development
Group relations
Trust, sensitivity
Communication;
Self-disclosure
Confidence building

P51   **Parent cocktail party**

Materials   None

Aims   Identify parental attitudes, develop role-playing techniques

Procedure   Become one of your parents. Pretend you are at a party.
                Move around the room, talking to the people you meet about
                your child (or children). Be sure you talk to many different
                people and listen to them as well. Return to the circle: do a
                round of 'I discovered ....'

Variations 1 Sit in a circle and make the parental statements as a round

                2 Be your other parent. Be you, discussing your parents

                3 Be a favourite teacher, then a much-disliked teacher

                4 Values continuum on relationships with parents

P52   # Projections ahead

Materials   None

Aims   Self-validation

Procedure   Each person envisages themselves at a particular point in the future. They think how life will be for them and using other members of their group, take turns in relating how they see themselves. Leader chooses their point in time, e.g. five years, ten years, etc. and also orientation, e.g.

a with family
b at work, etc.

The leader must state clearly whether this activity is to be as the person sees himself really, or as he wishes himself to be. If the leader thinks group comment is valuable, then care must be taken to ensure that the comments are positive and not demeaning.

Variations   1 Groups could develop one or more of their ideas into an improvisation.

2 Projections can be written down, discussed: could be national or world projections — including the person.

Personal development
Social development
Confidence building
Trust sensitivity
Communication,
Self-disclosure

P53   **Road map**

Materials   Large sheet of paper per person and pencil or felt tip

Aims   Self-validation

Procedure   Each person is asked to make a road map of their life so far,
beginning with birth and extending to the present. Each map
should somehow show the good places (either scenic or open
road, etc.) or the bad places (bumpy spots, etc.), hospital
(road works etc.) Also barriers, detours, and the general
direction of their present course.

Compare life's past course with your imagined future, i.e.,
goals, etc. How will they be achieved? What has made the
good spots?

Variations   1 Extend and project the map into the future. (conjecture or
daydream)

2 Construct lists of positive and negative problems and events.
Decide on points systems, i.e., + and −, and evaluate your
life.

3 Role play passing detours, etc.

Personal development
Communication,
Self-disclosure
Trust, sensitivity
Confidence building

P54 **Speakeasy**

Materials One chair

Aims Self-validation, group development

Procedure A chair is placed in front of the group. Each person has a chance to sit on the chair and talk to the group. They can develop any subject of their choice. It is often better to start out with descriptions of themselves — group leader setting the pace by going first.

This is a very important activity which can become a permanent feature of each drama lesson, especially if a drama lesson is over 60 minutes long.

Positive developments can result in group discussion and ways of resolving problems.

Variations Speak on controversial subjects, give views, then discuss, argue, do values continuum, etc.

P55

This is your life

Materials   None

Aims   Self-disclosure, trust building, role-playing, lead up to
                  improvisation.

Procedure   One person volunteers to be the director, and selects a story
                  from his own life, which he tells to the group. The group
                  then re-enacts the scene, under the director's supervision.
                  Discuss, then choose a new director.

Variations   If the group knows each other well, people can tell and direct
                  scenes from other people's lives.

P56 **Turning points**

Materials None

Aims Self-validation

Procedure Each person is asked to remember a particular point in their past. They remember what happened at that particular point and using other members of their groups, take turns relating this experience. The leader chooses the particular point, e.g. something that happened .... 5 years ago, and the orientation, e.g.:

a with family
b with friends
c at school, etc.

The leader may ask for the most important point in their lives. If the leader thinks that group comment is valuable, then care must be taken to ensure that the comments are sympathetic, constructive and understanding.

Variations Groups could develop one or more of these into an improvisation. This can be constructed as in 'Statues', or in which ever way the group wants to do it. A time limit is advisable. Ideas can be written down and evaluated in groups.

Personal development
Communication,
Self-disclolsure
Trust, sensitivity
Social development
Confidence building

P57   **Uniqueness cards**

Materials   One card or piece of paper for each person, pencils

Aims   Self-validation, communication, other-awareness

Procedure   Each person is given a card or piece of paper and asked to
                     write a description of themselves. The description must be
                     written in such a way that it could be no other person in
                     the group. It is better to describe ideas and personality
                     rather than physical appearance. Each person reads their
                     description out to the group. There will probably be many
                     descriptions which are not particularly unique. Have the
                     members of the group revise their descriptions and find out
                     how they really are unique. Goal is that no-one could say
                     'That's just like me!'

Variations   Write a card for someone else.

P58   # Value continuum

Materials   None

Aims   Self-validation, values clarification, communication, reflective listening.

Procedure   Leader and group decide on the subject to be evaluated. Subjects might be:

tidiness — untidiness
school's great — school's lousy
eat anything — very choosy
miser — spendthrift
T.V. always — T.V. never
wants no friends — wants everyone to be their friend
decision maker — decision avoider
100% happy — 100% unhappy
never argue — always argue
always follows others — individualist

Note   **topics can be much more sophisticated than the ones shown above**

One corner of the room is designated for the people of one extreme point of view and the next corner for the people of the opposite extreme view. Each person is then invited to place themselves, according to their opinion or practice, somewhere along the imaginary scale of degrees, on or between the two extremes. If two or more people wish to share the same point they can queue or sit outwards from the wall.

This 'declaration' can be used for discussion. As in other games no criticism is to be made of the person's choice.

Variations   1   Each person chooses where he would like to be, not necessarily where he would be in reality.

2   Each person explains why they are choosing a particular point.

3   Split continuum into two and have a dialogue between the two sides on 'why we are right!'

P59

Walk my walk

Materials　　　None

Aims　　　Self-awareness, observation, lead up to movement

Procedure　　　Stand in a large circle, leaving plenty of space in the middle. A volunteer walks across the circle several times, others observe his walk and comment on it. (Be sure comments are supportive and analytical: e.g. 'His shoulders are straight, his arms don't swing', etc.) Now everyone tries his walk, trying to really get into the feeling of being that person. Give as many volunteers a turn as possible, while interest holds.

Variations　　　Take on roles and walk in them: spy, aged person, jellyfish, etc.

Concentrative development

Contents

C60 **Addabout**

Materials None

Aims Concentration, memory, mime techniques

Procedure Sit in a circle. Leader stands, makes one simple movement, e.g.; spiral movement with finger. Next person makes spiral movement plus another, e.g. foot stamp, etc., adding while continuing around the circle. No talking, if someone misses or talks, he's out.

Variations Have the group invent a new rule

C61   # Add your emotions

Materials   None

Aims   Inter-personal development, improvisation

Procedure   Each group decides on a theme for a short improvisation. They then choose (or are given) three emotions to include in the story, so that the story progresses from the first emotion, through to the second, and finishes on the third.

e.g. worry .... panic .... relief (theme: fire)

When the groups work through the improvisation, and develop their ideas physically, they then develop three tableaux, each representing the emotion concerned. When the tableaux are shown to the whole group they should show the story seen in three 'frozen' pictures each demonstrating the particular emotion apparent at the point of the story. The story must also be apparent so that the tableaux also represent: *beginning, climax, conclusion.*

Some themes   a fire
watching a football game
a fight
attacked by a lion
ski-ing for the first time
themes basically invented by groups

Some emotions

pain	amusement	terror
pleasure	displeasure	fright
contempt	astonishment	loathing
weariness	indifference	degradation
triumph	impatience	alarm
horror	grief	worry
fear	excitement	shame
hatred	relief	

Variations   Choose themes from group suggestions. Let them decide emotions.

Concentrative development
Movement, body skills
Drama training
Communication
Social development
Trust, sensitivity

C62   **Adverb game**

Materials   None

Aims   Spontaneous reactions, imagination, fun, improvisation

Procedure   One person leaves the room, others choose an adverb, e.g.
                  'slowly'. When he returns he must find out what the adverb
                  is by asking people to do things 'that way', e.g. 'Shake hands
                  that way', (so they would shake hands very slowly.) If you
                  don't want to, or can't do what he says, you say 'I don't
                  want to', (very slowly). After each command he makes a
                  guess at the word: he can continue until he guesses or gives
                  up.

Variations   Leader calls out adverbs, e.g. 'nervously', and everyone
                  moves around the room that way. (This is good as a follow-
                  up activity, and to move into an active game or drama.)

C63   # Blind explore

Materials   None (blindfolds could be used)

Aims   Sensory awareness, trust building, warming-up in new group

Procedure   Darken the room if possible and also close eyes. Move
slowly, gently around the room. (No talking: emphasize it is
non-verbal). As you meet people gently greet them non-
verbally and move on. Now stop in front of someone:
explore their face. Allow a long time for this. Say goodbye
non-verbally, move on. Continue with the same directions,
and others: e.g. explore hands, play games with hands, be
angry and fight with hands — now make up, explore backs,
hair, etc. End with group hug in the centre.

Variations   See other blind games. Explore the room and allow
inanimate objects in it.

C64 **Blind find**

Materials None (darkened room)

Aims Trust building, fun, breaking down barriers, sensory awareness.

Procedure Darken room, everyone stand, (furniture pushed out of the way), close eyes. Begin gently moving around, walking slowly, no talking, when you meet people greet them non-verbally, gently, and move on. Leader gives series of instructions, gives plenty of time to experience each:

a Find someone with hair the same length as yours. When you find him take his hand and stand still. Someone else may join you if his hair is also the same. After plenty of time, open your eyes and check out your choice — is it really the same?

b Find someone with feet as big as yours

c Find someone with arms the same length as yours

d Find someone with a nose like yours

e Invent more things to find. (Clothes, mouths, hands.......)

C65   **Blindfold walking**

Materials   Blindfolds for half the group (optional)

Aims   Trust, concentration, self validation

Procedure   One person is blindfolded, or closes eyes, the other gives
                verbal instructions. The director is not allowed to touch the
                directed. (Change roles). It is a good idea to use a chair as a
                starting and a finishing point. Vary speeds. Obstacles placed
                in areas and the process repeated.

Variations 1 Races between pairs can be given and times
                2 Directions given by sounds only, e.g. one buzz for walk, two
                   buzzes for stop, etc. Try for variations of sound.

C66   **Bus**

Materials   Chairs set up as bus, tall stool for the driver

Aims   Improvisation, role playing, fun, group interaction

Procedure   First practise 'riding' on bus, let someone be the driver, call stops, make turns, etc. Passengers practise jolting along, leaning for turns, lurching at stops, etc. Then have all passengers adopt a role and maintain it, getting on and off the bus, talking to the driver, passengers sitting next to them, etc. Suggest the roles if necessary: lost old lady, man carrying bags of smelly rubbish to the dump, woman in a hurry, etc. Begin developing incidents involving everyone, such as hijacking, accident, drunks on bus, man wearing monkey suit gets on bus, etc.

Variations   Have passengers introduce themselves in role, give auto-biography. Bus could be aeroplane.

C67 **Chain mime**

Materials   None

Aims   Improve miming skills, concentration, memory training, fun

Procedure   Five people are chosen to leave the room — the group decides on a mime sequence for them to do, e.g. making a complicated sandwich, or changing a baby's nappy.

a is called in and told what to do

b is then called in and watches while **(a)** mimes changing the baby

c is then called in, and **(b)** repeats what he saw **(a)** do.

c repeats the mime for **(d)**, **(d)** repeats for **(e)**,

e mimes it for the audience. (The usual result is that the mime changes with each repitition, so that **(e)** is doing something *entirely different*). Ask each person what he thought he was doing.

Variations   Have each person deliberately add something new

C68   # Chain statues

Materials   None

Aims   Warm-up for movement, trust building

Procedure   One person takes a statue position in the centre. Another comes up and moves an arm or leg or hand, etc. The leader may say 'freeze' at any point, and everyone stays exactly where he is. Continue until the whole group is up.

Variations   See other statue games

Concentrative development
Warm-up, ice-breaking
Relax, winding down
Communication, contact

C69   **Chinese whispers**

Materials   None

Aims   Positive feedback, good for closing exercise

Procedure   Members mill around. When you see someone you'd like
to communicate with, send them a message via someone
else: e.g. 'Tell Joan I said thank you for helping me
yesterday.' Continue until messages run out.

Variations   Do as graffiti on large paper on walls. Do with bits of paper
being delivered. Do at a run, speed up, slow motion, etc.

C70 **Courtroom**

Materials   None (set up room like a court)

Aims   Improvisation lead-up, imagination, group team work, fun

Procedure   Phase one: Choose barristers, lawyers, judge, etc. as well as plaintiff and defendant. Send all of these out of the room. Improvise plaintiff being robbed or attacked by defendant, arrested by policemen, in front of audience. Have plaintiff and defendant meet with their lawyers, and get witnesses from audience. Hold trial, as much according to real procedure as possible.

Variations   Invent new crimes, change roles, adapt for mime/movement

C71   **Comic strip**

Materials   None

Aims   Improvisation, group development

Procedure   Each group develops an improvisation around a theme of its choice. When the improvisation is shown to the whole group, however, it is shown as a series of tableaux as in comic strip fashion.

Example   people on tube train

       Scene one: normal ride
       Scene two: train has lurched, passengers in disarray
       Scene three: back to normal

Variations   1   Take a well known story and depict in a series of tableaux

       2   Take a well known comic strip and parody it

Note   Limited conversation may be added, as long as there is no movement about the scene.

C72 **Clockwork people**

Materials   None

Aims   Concentration, movement, improvisation

Procedure   Each person becomes a clockwork figure who goes through a
complete performance when wound up. Leader should
perhaps denote a particular length for the sequence which
could be marked by suitable music. Emphasis should be given
on starting and finishing points. Can be co-ordinated into
Swiss clock, or group of robots, etc.

Variations   Develop so that action can be repeated exactly within a given
time.

C73   **Comparisons & opposites**

Materials   None

Aims   Improvisation, movement

Procedure   Work in pairs or teams: use mime or short improvisations

Compare   silence with noise, running with slow motion (really slow, almost imperceptible).
running and leaping with slow motion, exuberance with sorrow
old people — young people
tall people — short people
big (expansive and extrovert) — small (nervous and introvert)
floating — mud wallowing
sleek and darting — slow and ponderous
slow witted — quick witted
stiff person — loose person
rich — poor
strong — weak
industrious — lazy
taciturn person — chatterbox
Englishman — Frenchman
pompous person — friendly person
serious person — silly person
school teacher — school child
policeman — criminal
angel — devil
motorist — pedestrian
slow people — quick people

Variations   Development into improvisations: dealing with various situations; people might be involved in conversation, letter writing, shopping, etc.

C74 **Concentration points**

Materials   Needs silence

Aims   Concentration, movement sensitivity

Procedure   The following are improvisations which can be done
                  individually or in whatever relationship is desired.

                  Following a pattern on the floor (real or imaginary):

                  stepping stones
                  carrying full cups or glasses
                  walking over ice
                  walking on a tightrope
                  walking along a ledge
                  walking through a minefield in the dark
                  climbing a rockface
                  unwrapping a parcel secretly
                  applying eye make-up/war paint
                  watching a suspense drama
                  getting a poisonous snake in a box
                  extend into improvisations
                  wrapping a gift
                  decorating a cake
                  defusing a bomb
                  building a card house
                  safebreaking
                  throwing a ball
                  smoke writing
                  stealing
                  getting into a cinema seat
                  tieing a tie
                  threading a needle
                  getting into a suit of paper tissue

C75 **Control yourself**

Materials None

Aims Trust, body control, sensory awareness

Procedure The group is asked to lie down on their backs flat upon the floor, arms by their sides and their feet apart. Leader counts to ten (ten seconds approx.) during which time the group counts the number of inhalations and exhalations (i.e. total breaths) they make, (average about 5); this amount is increased so that the group can count ten or higher breaths in ten seconds. The amount can also be reduced to one per second or one per twenty, etc.

Variations
1 Control the speed of walking in the group. Walking very quickly/suddenly, contrasted by infinitely slow pace.

2 Group lies on stomachs and each person arches backs using stomach as a balancing point. Feet and shoulders must leave the floor. Leader establishes the length of each 'stretch'.

3 Each person stands with arms by sides, feet slightly apart. Without the help of the leader each person allows himself to sway in any direction. The point being to sway to severe angles but not allowing any over-balancing.

C76   **Emotions**

Materials   None

Aims   Emotional awareness, values development

Procedure   Leader asks group to characterise particular feelings or emotions, e.g.

pain	amusement	terror
pleasure	displeasure	fright
contempt	astonishment	loathing
weariness	indifference	degradation
honour	triumph	alarm
fear	loss	worry
hatred	excitement	shame
impatience	relief	

These emotions may be shown in a statue pose or moving or walking around. Sometimes it is good to include movement which the leader can freeze at will.

Variations   After striking a statue pose to represent a particular emotion the person is given six beats of a drum etc. to change fully into a different emotional stance.

Inter-relate with other emotions

C77   **Face touch**

Materials   None

Aims   Trust building, sensory awareness, easy lead-in to group
                  feeling. Best in group of 20 or more.

Procedure   Divide group into A's and B's. A's sit down in scattered
                  chairs, close eyes. No talking at all. Each B sits beside an A,
                  places A's hands on B's shoulders. A explores B's face, hair,
                  hands and shoulders. (Optional: A says positive sentences
                  starting: 'Now I am aware.......' e.g. 'Now I am aware that
                  your hair is soft, etc.') After a time, B stands and goes to
                  join the rest of B's in a line. A now opens eyes and goes to
                  find his partner in the line. A tells B how he identified him
                  in the line. Switch roles and repeat.

Concentrative development
Movement
Imagination, creativity
Drama training

C78 **Finish the action**

Materials None

Aims Improve mime skills, group interaction, imagination, lead up to improvisation.

Procedure One person begins to mime an action: e.g. surgeon operating on a patient. As soon as it is clear what he is doing, another (perhaps eventually the whole group) joins in: *non-verbal.* Continue until a natural ending is reached. Try to motivate the group to avoid easy/violent options for endings: e.g. blowing up the operating room.

Variations Add words, sounds

C79 **Fit the reader**

Materials   A magazine, newspaper or book

Aims   Imagination, fun, drama situations

Procedure   1 The leader chooses a piece of written material. Any paragraph, ordinary or otherwise.

2 He explains how each person in the group is to assume the role of a particular *kind* of reader.

3 The person is given the paragraph to read — without preparation — in the manner or style chosen by the reader.

Examples   in the manner of a horse racing commentator as the horses near the post.

in the manner of a children's story reader

in a style of a dignitary making a speech on a public occasion.

in a style full of insinuation and innuendo

in the style of a church minister or priest

in the manner of a suspicious policeman

C80   **Fun fair**

Materials   None

Aims   Improvisation, group development

Procedure   Whole group is split into half, then each half splits into
              smaller groups and develop different sideshows at a fun fair.
              When complete, one half act as members of the public who
              are visiting the fair while the other half try to attract people
              to their sideshows and let the people have a go. This
              situation is later evened so that the other side become the
              fair ground people.

              Ideas for
              sideshows:

              Shooting gallery
              Boxing display (have a go)
              Wall of Death
              Swings
              Darts
              Roundabouts
              One-armed bandits (fruit machines)
              Candy, toffee apples, etc.
              Coits
              The amazing ....
              Wrestling
              Juggling
              For sale
              Bingo

Variations   1 Develop the theme of 'The amazing........' Each exhibit
                 having something different and amazing to show.

              2 Do silently, develop into movement

C81   # Gibberish

Materials   None

Aims   Trust, personal development, expression

Procedure   The leader splits the group into pairs and suggests the point of a forthcoming conversation. It is then explained that no recognisable words will be used. The pair will talk as if in a foreign language, making up words and sounds. The point of the exercise is to develop in intensity of expression excluding real words.

Ideas for conversation

1 Lend me some money

2 Where were you last night?

3 Go home, your house has been burgled

4 It was the funniest game I've seen

5 Did you see that T.V. programme last night?

6 You've been brought here to talk and you'll tell us all we want to know.

Variations   Instead of sounds, or new words, numbers can be used

C82   **Group statues**

Materials   None

Aims   Warm up for movement, trust building

Procedure   Sit in a circle on the floor. One person takes a statue-like
                  position in the centre. The group names the statue. Another
                  person joins him, relating his own position to the original
                  statue. Give the new statue a name. Continue until the
                  group statue seems complete.

Variations   See other statue games

C83   **Guillotine**

Materials   Pencil and paper

Aims   Lead up to improvisation

Procedure   Partners decide on and write down six lines of conversation (three lines each). Use this as script. Now change the situation and repeat the same lines:

    a as if crossing the Sahara Desert

    b as if taking a man to the guillotine

    c as if you were two newlyweds at breakfast

    d any situation of your own choosing

C84   **Impersonations**

Materials   None

Aims   Improvisation, characterisation, group development

Procedure   Discuss what a parody entails. Each group decides which T.V. programme they are going to parody and spends about half an hour preparing their work. It is important that this is done properly and that when the groups show their work they are concerned with achieving humour through parody and not through other means. The group leader should help each group in its preparation where help is wanted and each parody must have a set length of time, i.e. 5 — 10 mins.

Variations   1 Famous sportsmen

2 Politicians

3 Local figures

C85   # Indian teepee

Materials   None

Aims   Concentration, fun, develop non-verbal expression

Procedure   Sit in a circle on the floor, each member chooses an Indian name and a non-verbal sign to go with it. (e.g. Falling Rain — ripple fingers in the air; Sleeping Papoose — close eyes, rock baby, etc.) From now on it is non-verbal. One member starts, makes his sign and someone else's. Whoever has the sign he's made, must respond immediately with that sign (his own) and someone else's, etc. If he doesn't respond immediately, he's out, and moves back out of the circle. The game should go very quickly. When only two are left, they try to get each other out.

Variations   Shout name while doing sign. Throw an object to the person whose sign you are making. Send other person's sign only, omitting your own.

C86   **Inside out**

Materials   None

Aims   Developing imagination, self-validation, sensory awareness, awareness, body control.

Procedure   Whole group lies on backs, arms on the floor, legs separate, eyes closed. Leader talks smoothly and steadily and asks the group to focus their senses within their bodies. Bodies are described as containing blood vessels with blood pulsing through; lungs exchanging oxygen for carbon dioxide (good air for used air); stomachs digesting food, etc. Group is asked to concentrate on one particular function of the body and the leader asks the group to be aware (even synthetically) of the existence of the activity, without feeling for signs with their hands.

'Real' sensations to notice
heartbeat
pulse
breathing
indigestion
digestion
perspiration, etc.

'Pseudo' sensations (to imagine entirely)
hair growing
nails growing
air in the blood
food passing to muscles
acids attacking the teeth, etc.

Variations   1   Concentration through breathing. Take a deep breath. Imagine your ribs expanding, the air rushing down your throat, filling your lungs, entering your blood and kicking the old air out. (continue with exhaling.)

                  2   Concentration through heartbeat. Blood sucked into one chamber — expelled into next chamber and then back into vein or artery. Concentration upon the feeling (in rhythm with the beats) of this expansion and contraction.

C87 **Killer**

Materials   Card pack

Aims   Concentration, eye contact, fun

Procedure   Sit in a circle, pass a card to each player, who peeks at it and keeps it hidden. Watch each other. Queen of Spades is the 'KILLER'. If he winks at you, you wait a few seconds, throw your card in the centre and say, 'I'm dead'. Do not tell who killed you. (Once you're dead, you can say nothing.) If you think you know the Killer, say, 'I accuse........' If you're wrong, you throw you card in: you have committed Suicide. Game ends when the Killer is discovered.

C88 **Look closer**

Materials Each person to have some ordinary object out, such as a pen, pencil, etc.

Aims To sharpen sensitivity and awareness and discover the uniqueness of everyday items.

Procedure Each person examines a small object, usually in everyday use, something simple like a pencil. Look it over very carefully and examine it closely. Then notice the over-all shape, any scratches, blemishes, any design or pattern; the leader tells his group to repeat the name of the object silently.

See if the name of the object seems inadequate

'Become the object': experience or try to describe what it is like to be that thing.

Introduce yourself to others

Concentrative development
Movement, body skills
Warm-up, ice-breaking
Relax, winding-down

C89   **Magic drum**

Materials   Drum and beater

Aims   Loosening-up, warming-up for movement

Procedure   Leader says: This is a magic drum, you can only move when you hear it beating. (beats) Move ..... freeze. (Repeat until they all freeze immediately at the stop of the drum beat.) Now the magic drum is even stronger, and you must move with the beat of the drum, but you must also move the way I tell you.

Be   spiky
jerky
smooth
faster
slower
old
young
melting like warm butter, etc.

Variations   Use piano or other rhythm instruments. Let a student use the drum.

C90 **Machines 1**

Materials   None

Aims   Concentration, group development

Procedure   One member of the group moves into a space and begins a machine-like movement. Each other member of the group joins the activity and 'develops' the machine. This can be done by linking in some way to the *action* of any of the people already in the machine. Music can be particularly helpful in this activity or each person could make a different sound for his action.

Variations   1 Machine could be joined into total group

2 Leader can choose machine tasks for groups

C91 **Machines 2**

Materials None

Aims Lead up to improvisation or movement, group decision-making, fun.

Procedure Divide into groups of 4 to 7 people, use the people to create a machine with moving parts. See that each person in the group is involved, either as part of the machine or operating it or being a product of it, etc. Show the machine to other groups.

Variations 1 add noises

2 assign a specific machine:

2.1 voodoo curse machine
2.2 laugh machine
2.3 juke box
2.4 trouble-making machine
2.5 insult machine

3 make a human development machine or a joy machine.

4 make a factory, using the large group

5 make a machine to suit purposes of group, e.g. primary education machine, etc.

C92 **The Mirror**

Materials   None (large empty space)

Aims   Concentration, silence, group togetherness, drama warm-ups, mime training, learning to observe.

Procedure   (First time). Stand in circle, watch leader, leader moves *very slowly,* using first just hands, then other parts of body and face. *Others move with him as in a mirror.* Stress slowness (raise hand to shoulder height on count of ten). Stress staying together. Illustrate difference between mirroring and following.

Variations   Do in pairs: watch partner's eyes while mirroring. Turn back on partner, listen to breathing, sense when partner is turning around, mirror the turn and movement. Work for total concentration. Take turns leading and mirroring, pass the leadership back and forth.

Give specific situations to mirror in two pairs.

Examples   barber and customer
milliner and customer
dress saleslady and customer

Sound mirror   watch partner's face closely,
mirror sounds.

C93   **Notice a colour**

Materials   None

Aims   Sensory development

Procedure   Choose one particular colour and notice that colour and all of its shades during the rest of the day. See how many shades you can give a name to.

Invent names

Choose a different colour and compare results with original colour.

Notice colour combinations. Look closely to see how many different colours go together and merge to make the overall shade. Check everyday items such as apples, book covers, etc. See how many colours are there. If you have chance, check an oil painting for the same qualities.

Variations   In group, place pieces of coloured paper on the floor. Each person chooses one, examines the colour, concentrates on it, 'becomes' that colour.

Write poetry or improvise around it.

C94   **Orchestration**

Materials   None

Aims   Concentration, group development

Procedure   Each member of the group decides upon one particular
method of producing a sound. Each person's sound should be
different from the next person's, etc. The main directive is
that it should be possible to produce the sound at will, and
also vary its strength. The leader then canvasses for a well
known rhythm of a particular tune and starts the group
humming the tune in unison. The leader then asks each
person in turn to continue the tune using their own
particular sound. It is up to the leader to decide whether
or not this is a totally individual effort, or whether the
background music continues. After each person has 'played'
once, the whole group 'orchestrates' the tune — every person
using their own individual sound at once. Leader can mimic
a real conductor by emphasising some sounds and reducing
others.

Variations   Invent own tunes.

Work in groups amplifying or balancing sounds for a better
effect.

C95   **Paper bag dramatics**

Materials   Characters written on cards (e.g. doctor, lift operator, bricklayer, etc.) and divided up with seven or eight in a bag.

Aims   Lead up to improvisation, group interaction, fun, imagination.

Procedure   Small groups, each one has a bag of characters, must use characters to create a scene. Share and evaluate scenes.

Variations   Combine with prop-building or proverb-building (C101 and C102).

C96   # Pass the object

Materials   None

Aims   Concentration, mime, fun

Procedure   Sit in a circle. Leader holds imaginary object, e.g. egg beater, and mimes using it for its purpose. He then passes it on to the next person, who 'uses' it, and then by making a rubbing motion with his hands, erases it and substitutes a new imaginary object, e.g. an ice-cream cone. Continue around the circle.

Variations   Leader 'uses' object, second person uses that one plus another, adding all the way the circle — this would make it a memory game.

Concentrative development
Trust, group interaction
Focal, concentration
Introductory, ice-breaker
Drama training

C97   **Pass the sound**

Materials   None

Aims   Sensory awareness, building feeling of group, concentration

Procedure   Stand in a circle, arms around each other (optional), close
                     eyes. Leader starts by making any sound (e.g. click tongue,
                     hum, etc.). Next person makes a sound of his own. Try
                     speeding up, slowing down, all at once, etc.

Variations   Spread out and hide around the room, experiment with
                     random sounds.

                     Try atmospheric sounds: sounds of forest, ocean, outer
                     space, farm.

                     Make a sound for every single movement or action: arm-
                     raising sound, jump-sound, etc.

C98 | **Photographers & models**

Materials   None

Aims   Concentration, self-validation

Procedure   Photographers place the person, including their features, into a pose that they feel representative of that person. Leader must explain how artists and photographers try to capture their models' personality and character in a pose. Models can resist.

Variations   Models decide how they would like to move. Photographers or models decide on the people they would like to be, or would like to copy.

C99   **Picture**

Materials   Pack of pictures

Aims   Improvisation, role-playing, social development and identity
                 awareness, etc.

Procedure   Leader shows picture or series of pictures on one particular
                 theme. The group discuss the implications seen in the scenes
                 and develop an improvisation based on the theme discussed.

Variations   Develop a similar situation by presenting smaller groups with
                 a picture each.

Note   in this activity more ideas should be drawn from the group
                 than should be given by the leader.

C100   **Polarities**

Materials   None

Aims   Concentration, movement

Procedure   Group acts out individual responses to contrasting forms, e.g.

spiky, *smooth*
angry, *placid*
heavy, *light*
small, *tall*
swamp creature, *drifting/floating creature/sky diver*
small moon, *huge planet*

Leader can add own ideas

Variations   1   In six beats of the drum grow from one form to its
contrasting opposite. (each polarity is a 'freeze' from a
statue).

2   Polarities are personified into people showing those
personality trends. Improvisations can be built on these,
working perhaps in pairs.

C101   **Prop-building**

Materials   Props, assorted

Aims   Lead up to improvisation, overcome shyness

Procedure   Divide into small groups, each group is given a prop, around
which to build a scene; e.g. an alarm clock, a treasure, a
telephone, etc. Share scenes and evaluate.

Variations   Give several props to each group, which must all be
incorporated in the scene.

Keep same prop, but change scene.

Concentrative development
Drama training
Imagination, — creativity
Movement, body skills
Warm-up, ice-breakers

C102 **Proverbs**

Materials None

Aims Improvisation, communication, group interaction

Procedure Each group is given one proverb as a starter for a timed
improvisation (or brainstorm your own). Leader should
discuss interpretation with each group beforehand.
Improvisation can be literal or developed in a symbolic
way; also in a mime or verbally.

A bird in the hand is worth two in the bush
A drowning man will clutch at a stone
A friend in need is a friend indeed
A rolling stone gathers no moss
A stitch in time saves nine
Absence makes the heart grow fonder
Actions speak louder than words
All that glitters is not gold
All's fair in love and war
Better late than never
Birds of a feather flock together
Blood is thicker than water
Charity begins at home
Discretion is the better part of valour
Don't put all your eggs in one basket
Don't count your chickens before they're hatched
Don't tell tales out of school
Empty vessels make the most noise
Every cloud has a silver lining
Forewarned is forearmed
It's an ill wind that blows nobody any good
It never rains but it pours
Look before you leap
Make hay while the sun shines
Many hands make light work
Necessity is the mother of invention

Variations 1 Are all proverbs true? Show

2 Can you think of any conflicting proverbs? Show

3 What or why proberbs? What purpose? Discuss

4 Make your own. Show

C103   # Remember

Materials   None

Aims   Concentration, memory

Procedure   Everyone studies the room and the people in it. One person goes out and the group changes something or someone. 'It' must come back in and try to find out what's changed.

Variations   1 Add something instead

2 Do in pairs, study each other, turn backs, change something.

Concentrative development
Drama training
Introductory
Warm-up, ice-breaker
Movement, body skills

C104   **Sentence themes**

Materials   None

Aims   Improvisation, characterisation, social development

Procedure   Each group is given one sentence theme as a starter for a timed improvisation. The sentence must be used by one of the characters in the play either as opening or closing line.

'Pass the salt'
'I wonder if I dare ask my boss for a rise?'
'He loses his temper so easily'
'Nobody in this house ever listens to me'
'Why can't you get home on time?'
'I don't want you out on the streets after dark'
'I spent the whole afternoon cooking dinner and none of you have eaten a thing'
'Hey, darling, I've some bad news for you'
'I've been hearing things about you'
'I always knew that would happen'

Variations   Develop into class drama: examine motives, etc. Combine some sentences. Brainstorm opening sentences. Explore the idea that without conflict or a problem there is no drama.

C105   **Silence is fragile**

Materials   Space and silence

Aims   Sensory awareness, self-validation, concentration

Procedure
1 Each member of the group (a) lies down on the floor with eyes closed.
or (b) sits crosslegged with eyes closed.

2 Leader asks for complete silence, and no contact between people

3 The group is then asked quietly to notice how calm and quiet everything is.

4 Each person then has to *think* of a particular exclamation (such as a scream) which would tear this silence in two.

5 After a minute the leader explains how he will touch each person in turn and as soon as they feel this touch they literally leap out across the room uttering the cry and return just as suddenly to their silent pose wherever they 'land'.

6 The leader must wait for complete calm before touching the next person.

C106   **Silent movies**

Materials   None

Aims   Concentration, improvisation, group development, development of basic elements.

Procedure   This type of improvisation can be used as either a starter or as a development of another improvisation. The point is to exaggerate the action involved with the improvisation and ideally to reduce complicated ideas into basic themes.

Improvisation must be 'shown' to effect with simplicity of form. Any theme can be used.

Examples   Parodies of various manner of film and plays, e.g. spies, romantic, thrillers, 40s movies, etc.

Concentrative development
Drama training
Movement, body skills
Introductory
Warm-up, ice-breaker

C107 **Situation**

Materials None. (Could have situations painted on cards)

Aims Lead up to drama, improvisation

Procedure Divide in small groups, give each group a situation, e.g. waiting in a maternity ward, trapped in an elevator, etc. Show improvisations one by one. Then take the same situations, change the characters involved and repeat. Share scenes and evaluate.

Variations Trade situations among groups. Let each group do the same situation but with different characters.

C108   **Sound detectives**

Materials   Pencil and paper

Aims   Memory training, concentration, sensory awareness

Procedure   Lead up: close your eyes and listen. What's the nearest
sound you can hear? The loudest? The softest? The
farthest away? Now the leader walks softly around the
room, making a series of sounds, about five to start with,
(e.g. click a scissor, leaf through a book, etc.) Members open
eyes and list the sounds they heard, in order. Check them
and discuss the experience.

Variations   Keep lengthening the list of sounds, make weird and un-
identifiable sounds. Let pupils take turns making sounds.

Concentrative development
Movement, body skills
Introductory
Drama training
Trust, group interaction

C109   **Statues**

Materials   None

Aims   Warm up for movement or drama, trust building

Procedure   Choose partners, designate A and B. A stands still but
                  relaxed, B moulds him, as though he were a lump of clay, in
                  into a statue. When you are finished, walk around and look
                  at the other statues. If you see something you'd like to
                  change, change it. Return to your own statue and decide
                  whether to leave it as it is, or change or restore it. Give it a
                  name. Share names or ideas aloud. Switch and repeat.

Variations   See other statue games

C110　　　　**Statue groups**

Materials　　None. A tambour or drum can be used however

Aims　　Concentration, group development

Procedure　　Group works out a statuary tableau

Ideas

from history	family life
mythology	school life
television	hospital
films	etc. etc.
famous stories	
great inventors	

Variations　　Each group viewed by others in turn. After each group has been viewed by the other groups, the tableau can be incorporated into an improvisation. The improvisation can begin from the tableau or end with the tableau. Set a time limit on each improvisation.

C111   **Still pond**

Materials   One blindfold

Aims   Trust building, sensory awareness

Procedure   Blindfolded person in the centre. Everyone else moves around until he says, 'Still Pond'. He moves forward and explores a face, guesses who it is. If he guesses, takes off blindfold, if not, he tries again.

Variations   As he moves forward, people make music or noises, while he searches for a specific person. (He might say 'I'm going to find David, etc.')

C112   **Story wheel**

Materials   None

Aims   Imagination, build group feeling

Procedure   Group lies down on their backs in wheel formation, heads
                   to the centre, one person starts story, next one continues,
                   etc. Try to create mood or atmosphere to fit story.

Variations   Sit in circle, have storyteller walk around and act out story
                   before passing it on.

C113   **Toyshop**

Materials   Darkened room, lighting or candles, piano or other music, – optional.

Aims   Improvisation, discovery of talent, movement, fun, – adults enjoy this as much as children.

Procedure   Brainstorm kinds of toys which move. Become various toys and move around room. Stop, start, and trade toys (roles). Choose roles for the improvisation: toymaker, two robbers, policeman, toy soldiers, other toys. Leader tells story, group acts it out. Story in brief: an old toymaker tries out his toys, then locks up the shop and goes home. The toys come alive at midnight and play. Two robbers steal into the shop, seeking the toymaker's savings. As they are about to find the money, toy soldiers come in, capture and tie them up; in the morning, toymaker returns, finds robbers, calls policeman. He will never know who captured the robbers.

Variations   Have students invent new toys, new story.

Other directed improvisations:
wax museum
art gallery
clock shop
history museum
department store at midnight

C114   **Travel agent**

Materials   None

Aims   Improvisation, imagination, fun

Procedure   Divide into groups of 3 — 4. Choose roles: travel agent and
              types of customers. Develop roles by asking for ages, sexes,
              types, problems, of customers and agents. Improvise plays in
              travel bureau, which could include time travel, space travel,
              etc. Share improvisations. Evaluate.

Variations   Do as a whole group

C115   **Treasure chest**

Materials   4 or 5 chosen objects

Aims   Develop imagination, improvisation

Procedure   Leader shows four or five objects separately to the whole
                     group. Each object is discussed as to its possible or projected
                     uses. Members of the group can step forward and show how
                     the object could be used. (This both clarifies use and after
                     use allows individual development of ideas). Eventually
                     group is split into small groups and each group is given an
                     object around which to build an improvisation. The
                     improvisation may be shown afterwards.

Ideas for objects   long broom handle (spear, etc.)
                     large piece of plain cloth
                     simulated parchment (map)
                     large plastic ring
                     a heavy key
                     old transistor radio
                     cardboard/paper tube
                     handkerchief (with initial)
                     decorated goblet or crown
                     empty film canister

Variations   Individuals try to auction the objects which are shown.

C116   **Vibrations**

Materials   None

Aims   Self-validation, inter-personal development

Procedure   In pairs:

    a Bring your two hands close to your partner's two hands, (palm to palm) until they are almost touching.

    b Close eyes and experience the sensation of warmth or energy

    c Experiment with distances

Variations   1 Try blindfold — discuss effect

    2 Use faces instead of palms

    3 Do in a circle.

C117   **Wax museum**

Materials   None (costumes, optional)

Aims   Improvisation, concentration, imagination, fun

Procedure   Brainstorm famous figures to appear in wax museum, some
in groups. Try being the still figures, add costume if desired.
Have students invent story about wax museum, e.g. sculptor
uses real people for figures, etc. Improvise the story.

Variations   Change story

C118   # What can you feel?

Materials   None

Aims   Sensory development, concentration

Procedure   Each person is asked to notice particularly the textures they can feel. In this activity the leader must classify the group's surroundings in such a way that they can report small groups of objects noted particularly. Each person or small group may be given separate classifications to seek out, or the group as a whole may be set each classification in turn. Group may suggest its own classification.

Ideas for classification

rough	turns	sticky	hard
smooth	splintery	wet	prickly
sharp	gritty	dry	spongy
cold	woven	delicate	squelchy
cool	soft	silky	sturdy
warm	coarse	scratched	hot
crumbly	etc.		

Discuss afterwards why they include particular objects in their classifications.

Variations   1   Compare interior textures with exerior ones

             2   Run to each article when it is named.

             3   Pass objects around for blindfolded experience.

C119   # What can you hear?

Materials   None

Aims   Sensory development, concentration

Procedure   Whole group either:

             a lie down on the floor with eyes closed
or   **b** sit crosslegged with eyes closed.

Leader asks for *complete* silence and stresses there be no contact during the time set. During this time each person listens very carefully and counts and remembers every single sound they can hear. At the end of the activity each member lists the things that they heard — or a list is compiled from the class as a whole.

Discuss which sounds are most audible, and likes and dislikes, etc.

Variations   Compare the sounds of an interior room with the sounds outside the building.

C120   **What can you see?**

Materials   None

Aims   Sensory development, concentration

Procedure   Each person is asked to notice particularly the things they can see. In this activity the leader must classify the group's surroundings in such a way that they can report small groups of objects noted particularly. Each person or small group may be given a separate classification to seek out, or the group as a whole may be set and asked to classify in turn. Group may suggest classification.

Ideas for classifications (each may be going through inter-mediary classification, too.)

distant, *near*
huge, *tiny*
reds, blues, yellows, *tones, etc.*
colourful, *drab*
horizontal, *vertical*
straight, *rounded*
even, *uneven*
delicate, *sturdy*
shiny, *dull*
light, *dark*
outstanding, *obscure*
natural, *artificial*
plain, *patterned*
interesting, *boring*

discussion afterwards on why they chose particular classifications.

Variations   1   Compare the abundance of one classification inside or outside

2   Run to each article when it is named.

C121 ## What is it?

Materials   One chair for each group

Aims   Improvisation

Procedure   Each group takes one inanimate object such as a chair, or a broom, etc., and each person uses it in a different way, e.g. a chair could become a wheelbarrow, a horse, a crate, a sleigh, etc. etc. Try to develop as many strange uses as possible.

Variations   More than one person may be used to demonstrate a particular use.

C122   **Who am I?**

Materials   None

Aims   Improvisation; imagination

Procedure

a Each person chooses to become a famous character either from history, entertainment, literature, government, etc.

b Leader asks each person to sit separately and concentrate on:

b1   the kind of personality the character has.

b2   their mannerisms.

b3   the way they talk.

b4   what they say.

c When everyone is ready they can stand up as the character they have chosen and move around to introduce themselves to each other.

d They can also hold conversations with one another making sure they retain all the characteristics of the famous person.

C123   # Who started the motion?

Materials   None

Aims   Concentration, trust building

Procedure   Circle; one person (A) leaves. Leader chooses someone to
                   start the motions such as slapping, tapping feet, waving, etc.
                   Everyone watches the starter and changes motions when he
                   does, while appearing not to watch him. 'A' has to guess who
                   the starter is.

Variations   Use blindfold and change sounds instead of motions.

Introductory games

Contents

I124 **Famous people**

Materials Famous names on strips of card or paper, straight pins. Could be real people (Joan ot Arc), tictional (Superman), etc.

Aims Mixing, starting conversation, ice-breaking

Procedure As people enter, leader pins a name on each person's back. Each one must walk around and try to find out who he is by asking yes-or-no questions of everyone else. When he knows who he is, he pins the paper on his front and continues to help others.

Variations Try it non-verbally. Try insisting that everyone must make statements (e.g. 'I am alive'), and no questions allowed.

I125   **Getting to know you**

Materials   None

Aims   Introduction, memorizing names

Procedure   Whole group is spread over area. At a given signal they must move around and shake hands with as many people as possible. With every handshake they are introducing themselves; each person should try to remember as many names as possible. The leader must make every effort to establish a *real* introduction and not an empty one.

I126   **Group fantasy trip**

Materials   None

Aims   Relexation, build group feeling, inspire creativity, imagination

Procedure   Stretch out comfortably, close eyes, concentrate on breathing. Let imagination roam. When an image comes clearly to mind, speak out and describe it. Others listen, feel free to add to images, without interrupting. Continue as long as it seems rewarding, allowing long silences when they develop.

Variations   Add soft music. Draw or paint images as they occur. Dance or improvise fantasies. Do gentle massage during fantasies.

I127 # Move to the spot

Materials   Large, empty room or space

Aims   Learning to follow simple instructions, movement, warm-up for Drama

Procedure   Leader says: 'Find a place to stand by yourself. Now look at and concentrate on a fixed spot on the floor, somewhere across the room. Now, move to that spot in a straight line, pacing yourself so as not to have to stop, while avoiding bumping into anyone.'

Leader continues to give similar instructions, allowing time for individuals to (A) concentrate on each spot, (B) move at their own pace, and (C) settle into the new spot.

Instructions for (B) could include moving to the new spot:

1   backwards
2   in as few steps as possible
3   in as many steps as possible
4   travelling in circles
5   travelling in squares
6   using as few jumps as possible
7   with hands on knees, toes etc.
8   moving along floor without using hands
9   with a partner, using only two out of four legs
10 reflecting various emotions, e.g., fear, etc.

Variations   Have group invent more instructions.

I128

How do you like your neighbour ?

Materials   Chairs

Aims   Exercise, warm-ups, fun

Procedure   Chairs in a circle. Number each person, 1, 2, 3, 4 etc. One person in centre, remove one chair. The centre person points to someone and says 'How Do You Like Your Neighbour?'

There are two ways to answer:

a *'I like him'.* In this case, everyone gets up and moves to another chair. Last one standing is in the centre next.

b *'I don't like him'.* In this case, centre person asks 'Who do you want?'. The answerer calls any two numbers — the two people on his right and left must move, and the two people with the numbers called must try to get their chairs.

b2 When asked 'Who do you want?', the answerer says: 'Nobody', then everyone *except* the answerer runs around the outside of the circle, until the answerer says 'Stop'. Everyone then goes for a chair.

Variations   Invent new answers with the group

I129

Human noughts & crosses (Tic-Tac-Toe)

Materials   9 chairs, running space

Aims   Active participation, warm-up, fun

Procedure   At one end of the room, three rows of three chairs each, four feet apart. Teams: Team 1 is 'Noughts', Team 2 is 'Crosses'; they line up in corners of the room facing the chairs. When the leader calls 'noughts', the first nought runs to a chair and sits with arms circled above head. Runner must sit before Leader counts to 5 slowly. Leader calls 'crosses', first cross runs and sits with arms crossed on chest. Leader continues to call them alternately until one team wins (same rules as paper Noughts and Crosses). Start over, call losing team first. Keep score (optional).

Variations   For more active warm-up, do outside with long running space.

I130   **Identifipicture**

Materials   None

Aims   Indentity. Warm-up

Procedure   One person in the group stands with their back to the group
                   and another person describes someone in the group. They
                   must be careful to describe each person in a positive way, and
                   not in a fashion which could be seen as derogatory. There is a
                   time allowance during which the person has to guess who is
                   being described. The person out front has then to choose
                   another person to come out front and the former then
                   chooses someone else to describe.

Variations   The person at the front asks questions instead of just giving
                   answers.

I131   **Man the ship**

Materials   None — large room

Aims   Warm-up, exercises, fun, concentration

Procedure   Group forms one line (single file) down the centre of the room. If the Leader shouts, 'Man the Starboard' — everyone runs right. If the Leader shouts, 'Man the Port' — everyone runs left. 'Man the Ship' means back to the centre. Leader shouts commands faster and faster: last person to arrive at any line is out. Eliminate until one person wins.

I132   **Mill & grab**

Materials   None

Aims   Form groups, mix people, be active

Procedure   Mill around. Leader calls number (e.g. '5'), members run to
                make circles of 5, holding hands up together. Those left over
                go to one spot, perhaps can form another group. Leader
                waits until all the groups are ready, then calls another
                number, e.g. '2', '25', etc. (If the leader wants groups of 7
                for the next game, he stops with 7, tells groups to keep their
                7 and sit down). Emphasize that groups must be mixed,
                boys and girls, teachers and pupils, etc.

Variations Do with eyes closed. Do in silence. Do in slow motion. Do as
                noisily as possible. Do according to an adverb, e.g. childishly,
                etc.

I133   **The name of the game**

Materials   One ball for every group of about 15 — 16.

Aims   Introduction, memorizing names

Procedure   New group sits in a circle of not more than sixteen. One
person is given a ball. The ball is passed around the circle
and each person who receives the ball says their name very
clearly (usually just the first name). When everyone has been
named and the ball is back to the beginning, the person
holding the ball throws it to any person. That person must
say the thrower's name. The ball is then thrown to someone
else who must say the next thrower's name. If a person
cannot remember the name of the person who has thrown
the ball to him, they must ask and repeat the name before
proceeding with the activity. The game continues until
everyone can remember the names of the people within their
group. Group size is usually about sixteen.

I134   # Persuasion

Materials   Chocolate bars (about one for every five people), or any
                     similar prize.

Aims   Test imagination and powers of persuasion

Procedure   Select three judges, give them time to design a points system.
                     Each student comes before the judges, one by one, and tries
                     to convince them that he should deserve a chocolate bar.
                     Points should be awarded for originality and persuasiveness.

Variations   Do in writing; make an improvisation where the judges are
                     bribed, etc.

I135   # Sherlock Holmes

Materials   Items in possession, pencil and paper

Aims   Get acquainted, trust building

Procedure   Take six items from handbag, person, or pocket, show them
                   to your partner. Do not talk. Write down what you have
                   deduced about your partner from looking at his belongings.
                   Share your deductions with the group, and get a response
                   from your partner as to how accurate they are.

Variations   Put everyone's items on a table — decide what belongs to
                   whom, and why.

I136   **Simon says**

Materials   None

Aims   Concentration, fun

Procedure   Each group chooses a leader who leads by performing actions
to be imitated by the rest of the group, before each section
the leader says:

'Simon says — Put your hands on your head'.

If the leader gives any order without the prefix 'Simon says',
the group should not imitate the action or follow the order.
If any member makes a mistake he leaves the group until the
end of the activity. This activity is better if speed is
emphasised.

Variations   1   Change leaders

2   Think of ways to make it more difficult.

I137   **Squeeze & stretch**

Materials   None

Aims   Relaxation, body control, sensory awareness

Procedure   Each person sits on the floor with their knees drawn up, arms are clasped tightly around their legs, heads buried in their knees, back arched tightly; calves, thighs, buttocks, neck, fists, feet, — all clenched: shoulders forward and around legs, face muscles tightened — every muscle contracted and tightened. Hold that position for at least a minute and then very slowly release and unwind until your body is really spread and relaxed. Then each person immediately progresses to a stretching position when toes and fingers are spread, back arched, legs and arms extended fully, all joints are pulled apart (mention in turn, ankles, elbows, etc.): face is opened with wide eyes, tongue out, etc.

Now relax fully.

Discuss afterwards the awareness of tension. By deliberately creating tension and then relaxing, you can often alleviate tension received from outside sources.

I138   # Tangle

Materials   None

Aims   Group development, trust, warm-up

Procedure   Whole group links hands into a human chain. First person leads chain through itself, over and under arms, between legs, etc. Extra care must be taken not to break the chain, to move slowly and to be gentle. Tangle ends when group is too tightly packed to move. One person then untangles the group, giving them directions without touching them.

I139   # Tick tock

Materials   Two small different objects, such as a blue felt pen and a red felt pen.

Aims   Breaking the ice, concentration

Procedure   Leader has pen (or other object), passes it to his right, saying: 'This is a tick'. Player 1 says: 'A what?' Leader repeats: 'A tick'. 1 then passes it on saying, 'This is a tick'. Player 2 says: 'A what?' to player 1, who says: 'A what?' to the leader. Each time the 'What?' must pass all the way to the leader, and the 'A tick' must pass all the way back, before the pen is passed. When this has been practised a few times, start over, and at the same time, start another pen to the left, saying: 'This is a tock', etc. Confusion is encouraged and acceptable. Let the group try, as long as desired, to return both objects to the leader without losing the flow or concentration.

I140   # Two-minute autobiographies

Materials   None

Aims   Mixing, self-awareness, self-disclosure, trust building.

Procedure   Find a partner, preferably one you don't know at all. You have two minutes to tell them what you would especially like them to know about you and your life: past, present, hopes, plans, facts, etc. After each has a turn, join another pair, and introduce your partner to them, telling what you remember about their autobiography. When each of the four has had a turn, join the whole group and introduce your partner to them. Do a round of 'I learned'.

Variations   Stop with either the pairs or the foursomes and ask each other questions, letting the autobiographies grow deeper.